The Twelve Teas of Inspiration

Celebrations to Nourish the Soul

EMILIE BARNES
Paintings by SUSAN RIOS

HARVEST HOUSE PUBLISHERS
EUGENE, OREGON

The Twelve Teas® of Inspiration

Cover by Garborg Design Works, Savage, Minnesota
Interior design and production by Garborg Design Works

Original artwork © Susan Rios. For more information regarding artwork featured in this book, please contact:

> Susan Rios, Incorporated
> 15335 Morrison St., Suite 102
> Sherman Oaks, CA 91403
> (818) 995-7467 www.susanriosinc.com

THE TWELVE TEAS is a registered trademark of The Hawkins Children's LLC. Harvest House Publishers, Inc., is the exclusive licensee of the federally registered trademark THE TWELVE TEAS.

Copyright © 2007 Text © by Emilie Barnes; Artwork © by Susan Rios
Published by Harvest House Publishers
Eugene, Oregon 97402
ISBN-13: 978-0-7369-2016-2
ISBN-10: 0-7369-2016-1

Printed in Singapore

07 08 09 10 11 12 13 14 15 / IM / 10 9 8 7 6 5 4 3 2 1

CONTENTS

Tea's Legacy

Almost every day my mama had a freshly made pot of tea waiting for me when I came home from school. She owned a small dress shop and often would invite customers to join us for a cup of tea. The table was simply set with china teacups and saucers, a lit candle, and a small vase or jar with a few flowers. It was simple but very welcoming. I loved to hear the gentle voices and laughter of friends visiting. However, the happiest times were when it was just Mama and me sitting down for tea and conversation.

Tea inspires comfort during times of trial, friendship between neighbors and strangers, and peace during the busiest days. Tea brings people together and provides a way to give and receive and create community wherever we are and with whomever is near. It is even the perfect companion when we are alone and enjoying a time of devotion, prayer, or simple solitude.

Let's take the time to give other people hope and encouragement about life. Nothing of permanent value has ever been accomplished without inspiration. The themed teas in this book will provide a creative canvas for you to add the color and texture and wonder of your own personality and charm. Whether you set out two mismatched cups on a sun-warmed picnic table or a full tea service on a cloud of white linen, you will inspire joy and relationship in those around you.

May your cups be filled with love, peace, and inspiration...and may you share them soon with another.

Emilie Barnes

Emilie's Inspired Classics

*T*he twelve themed teas in this book provide numerous variations to spark your imagination and to give you new reasons to gather together old friends, new friends, neighbors, and relatives over pots of tea. Before we embark on variety, let us not forget the wonderful foundations of any tea—whether for yourself or a dozen people.

I encourage you to look at these classics and add your own unique touches—a special ingredient, a favorite flavor, a family tradition, or an unusual presentation.

The Inspired Pot Tea

Preparing a perfect cup of tea takes time, but the flavor and excellence is worth it!

- Fill a teakettle with freshly drawn cold water. Put the kettle on to boil.
- While the kettle is heating, pour hot water into the teapot to warm it. Ceramic (china, porcelain, stoneware) or glass teapots work best. Tea brewed in a metal teapot may have a metallic taste.
- Pour the hot water out of the teapot and add the tea. Measure a spoonful of loose tea for each cup desired into the warmed-but-now-empty teapot, plus one extra spoonful. (Most teapots hold five to six cups.) If you are using tea bags, use one bag less than the desired number of cups. Put the lid back on the pot.
- As soon as the kettle comes to a rolling boil, remove from heat. Overboiling causes the water to lose oxygen, and the resulting brew will taste flat.
- Pour boiling water into the teapot, cover, and let the tea brew from three to six minutes. Small tea leaves will take less time to brew than larger ones.
- Gently stir the tea before pouring it through a tea strainer into the teacups. If you used tea bags, remove them.

Favorite Tea Sandwiches

Cucumber sandwiches are perhaps most commonly associated with afternoon tea. Peel cucumbers and slice very thin. Sprinkle slices with salt and drain on paper towels. Spread white bread with unsalted butter and a thin layer of cream cheese. Layer cucumbers no more than ¼-inch thick. Cut into desired shapes.

Watercress sandwiches are also favorite tea-party fare. Butter white or rye bread. Layer on watercress leaves. Cut into squares, arrange on plate, and garnish with watercress.

Other tea sandwich ideas (place on white bread unless otherwise noted):

- Thinly sliced chicken breast or smoked salmon with watercress and mayonnaise.
- Bagel rounds (slice one bagel in horizontal thirds) with a spread of cream cheese, topped

with thin slices of smoked salmon, tomato rounds, onions, and capers.
- Stilton cheese crumbled over apple slices on pumpernickel bread.
- Cream cheese mixed with chutney, a dash of curry, and lemon juice.
- Paper-thin slices of red radish on white bread spread with unsalted butter.

Basic Scones

(makes 8)

    2 cups flour
    1 tablespoon baking powder
    2 tablespoons sugar
    ½ teaspoon salt
    6 tablespoons butter
    ½ cup buttermilk (or regular milk)
    1 egg, lightly beaten

Mix dry ingredients. Cut in butter until mixture resembles coarse cornmeal. Make a well in the center and pour in buttermilk or regular milk. Mix until dough clings together and is a bit sticky. Don't overmix! Turn out dough onto a floured surface and shape into a 6- to 8-inch round about 1½-inches thick. Quickly cut into pie wedges or use a large, round biscuit cutter to cut circles. The secret of tender scones is a minimum of handling. Place on ungreased cookie sheet, being sure the sides of scones don't touch each other. Brush with egg for a shiny, beautifully brown scone.

Bake at 425° for 10 to 20 minutes, or until light brown.

You can add all kinds of extras to scones, depending on your taste. Try cut-up apples, currants, ginger, orange, almond flavoring, cinnamon, apricots, fresh blueberries, cranberries, or even chocolate chips.

Mock Devonshire Cream

This is a delicious sweet cream for your scones.

    ½ cup heavy cream or 8 ounces softened cream cheese
    2 tablespoons confectioner's sugar
    ½ cup sour cream

In a chilled bowl, beat cream until medium-stiff peaks form, adding sugar during the last few minutes of beating. (If you are using cream cheese, just stir together with sugar.) Fold in sour cream and blend. Makes 1½ cups.

A New Beginnings Tea

Nourish beginnings, let us nourish beginnings.

Murial Rukeyser

Beginnings are a time of cheer, possibility, and hope. They're also the perfect time to celebrate. Is a friend embarking on a new marriage, starting a family, or venturing into a new job? Get your teacups ready! It's time to honor a new beginning.

One of my favorite beginnings to celebrate is a new home for a family, a couple, or friend. You can host this tea as a housewarming for the person at her new place, or you can host the gathering at your home. If this is a first home, when you send invitations it's wonderful to recommend that guests bring a gift from either a store registration list or from a list of items you know the person or family will need. If this is a merged household (for a marriage or blended family) or a second home, perhaps the best gift will be the gathering of friends to bless the new home and its new residents.

> *Start by doing what's necessary; then do what's possible; and suddenly you are doing the impossible.*
>
> St. Francis of Assisi

Serve a good quality tea at your party, accompanied by milk, lumps of sugar, and wedges of lemon. Try the recipes here or your own favorites.

9

Menu for a New Beginnings Tea

Turkey-Orange Sandwiches • Lemon Bites • Frosted Ruby Punch

Turkey-Orange Sandwiches

Thinly sliced roasted turkey breast
Orange marmalade
Small can mandarin orange slices
Rye bread, buttered

Place turkey on slice of buttered bread. Spread marmalade lightly on turkey. Top with more turkey and a slice of bread. Trim crusts and cut into triangles. Spear orange slice on top of each sandwich with festive toothpicks.

Lemon Bites

(serves 24)

Shells
1 cup all-purpose flour
½ cup finely chopped pecans
¼ cup sugar
1 egg
¼ cup softened butter (½ stick)

Filling
1 teaspoon unflavored gelatin
1 tablespoon cold water
2 eggs
½ cup sugar
2 tablespoons grated lemon zest
¼ cup fresh lemon juice
2 tablespoons butter
whipped cream
Additional grated lemon zest for garnish

For the shells, preheat the oven to 375° F.

Mix the flour, pecans, and sugar in a bowl. Add the egg and butter and mix until crumbly. Press the dough onto the bottoms and sides of ungreased miniature muffin cups. Bake for 10 to 12 minutes or until light, golden brown. Remove the pans to a wire rack to cool.

For the filling, soften the gelatin in the cold water in a saucepan.

Beat the eggs and sugar in a bowl. Stir into the gelatin mixture. Bring to a boil, stirring constantly.

10

Reduce the heat and simmer for 10 minutes. Remove from the heat, and stir in the lemon zest, lemon juice, and butter. Pour the filling into baked shells. Chill for 1 hour or until set.

Remove from the muffin cups to a serving platter. Garnish with whipped cream and lemon zest.

Frosted Ruby Punch

(makes 8 servings)

4 cups cranberry juice
1½ cups sugar
1½ cups lemon juice
1 cup orange juice
4 cups ginger ale (chilled)
1 quart raspberry sherbet

Pour cranberry juice into a 5-cup ring mold. Freeze overnight.

In a punch bowl, combine sugar, lemon juice, and orange juice until sugar is dissolved. Stir in ginger ale.

Remove ice ring from the mold and float in punch bowl. Place scoops of sherbet around ring.

> *Spread love everywhere you go: First of all in your own house…let no one ever come to you without leaving better and happier. Be the living expression of God's kindness: kindness in your face, kindness in your eyes, kindness in your smile, kindness in your warm greeting.*
>
> MOTHER TERESA

A Touch of Inspiration

For a housewarming, send a nicely designed, blank recipe card with the invitations and ask each guest to list ingredients for a loving home, such as "kindness and hospitality" or "lots of listening and laughter." The guests can read these aloud and then give them to the honored person or family at the tea as a way of celebration and support.

A Thankful Heart Tea

I will praise God's name with singing,
and I will honor him with thanksgiving.

Psalm 69:30

One of the great joys in life is to give thanks to God for all abundances of life. We can do it in prayer, in song, through grace, and in blessing. We can do it for every occasion, including births, dedications, housewarmings, graduations, weddings, and anniversaries. Life gives us a multitude of opportunities to say, "Thank You, Lord." Grateful hearts give thanks.

> *We thank You, Lord, for blessings*
> *You give us on our way;*
> *May we for these be grateful,*
> *And praise You every day.*
>
> ROWORTH

This *Thankful Heart Tea* is an occasion for praise. You can celebrate any event in your life or that of a friend by expressing thanks with a lovely tea. Make it as simple or detailed as you want it to be. You'll inspire others to embrace a heart of gratitude. Perhaps you'd like to host a tea just to thank your neighbors for the generosity they've expressed over time in the loaning of tools, babysitting of kids, picking up of mail. Show how much you appreciate them for being part of your life.

Maybe you have gone through a hard time and have relied on the goodness of friends...and even some people you didn't know very well before. *A Thankful Heart Tea* is

13

an opportunity to bring those people together as you lift up praise to God and appreciation to these friends for bringing you through a hard time. What a celebration this can be!

These days it's easy to get caught up in your family's immediate schedules and needs. Setting aside a time to express gratefulness is a way to step beyond those important but consuming tasks that occupy our days and our minds. Few things honor and glorify God more than the sweet fragrance of a thankful soul. Gratitude encourages graciousness.

Tea Delights

For a burst of citrus flavor, heat water with honey, a lemon slice, and a cinnamon stick. Add the tea bag. Or stir orange marmalade and a little lemon juice into a cup of brewed tea.

Menu for a Thankful Heart Tea

Filled strawberries • Cucumber Sandwiches • Spiced Tea

Filled Strawberries

These fresh-fruit treats are like strawberry cheesecakes in miniature—perfect for a festive tea.

6 ounces cream cheese, softened
½ teaspoon pure vanilla extract
1½ tablespoons confectioner's sugar
12 large strawberries
¼ cup sliced almonds

Whip 6 ounces of room-temperature cream cheese on medium speed until slightly puffy, about 2 to 3 minutes. Add ½ teaspoon pure vanilla extract and 1½ tablespoons confectioner's sugar. Trim tops and bottoms of 12 strawberries to level. Use small melon ball utensil to scoop out strawberries. Using a pastry bag with ½-inch star tip, fill with cream cheese mixture and pipe into berries until mixture brims over tops. Toast ¼ cup sliced almonds in a 350°F oven until golden brown, about 3 to 6 minutes. Arrange almonds on top of the filling.

Cucumber Sandwiches

See "Favorite Tea Sandwiches" on page 6 or create a variation of your own.

Spiced Tea

(makes 3 quarts)

 2 medium lemons
 2 teaspoons whole cloves
 7 tea bags, 1-cup size
 2 teaspoons whole allspice
 11 cups boiling water
 2 cups sugar
 1⅓ cup orange juice
 ⅔ cup lemon juice

Cut each lemon into 6 slices and stud slices with cloves. Put tea bags and remaining spices in boiling water in a large Dutch oven (any big kettle

I awoke this morning with devout thanksgiving for my friends, the old and the new.

RALPH WALDO EMERSON

will do). Cover and let steep over medium heat for 15 minutes. Remove tea bags and spices. Add sugar and orange and lemon juice. Pour tea mixture into heatproof serving bowl. Add lemon slices. Serve hot.

A Touch of Inspiration

Look up special prayers, Irish blessings, and quotes that suit the occasion of thanksgiving. Type up or write out several of them on nice paper and display them around your home and by the tea service as sweet reminders of ways to give thanks.

"A Thing of Beauty Is Forever" Tea

A thing of beauty is a joy forever.

John Keats

As we think, as we walk, as we read, as we visit with friends—hopefully our eyes and minds capture all the beauty that we experience. Creation abounds with evidence of a creative and loving Creator. I love all seasons because they each present a different glimpse of God's marvelous artistry. Beauty is not just in the eye of the beholder. Beauty is found in the expression of music that brings a listener to tears with its power and majestic melodies. There is beauty in how a writer presents images and ideas that are fresh, exciting, and intriguing casting life in a new light.

Use this special gathering as an opportunity to share the beauty of the ritual of tea while also honoring the beauty of your guests and

Beauty is the only thing that time cannot harm. Philosophies fall away like sand, and creeds follow one another like the withered leaves of autumn; but what is beautiful is a joy for all seasons and a possession for all eternity.

OSCAR WILDE

17

the way they experience loveliness and wonder in their lives. Encourage your guests to bring with them something of beauty. Maybe it will be a flower, or a child's handprint in orange paint, or a photo of a childhood home. What they bring might be a sweet memory of a special moment with a person. During the afternoon, give each lady an opportunity to share her object of beauty. You will all be inspired by the various items and ideas of what is to be adored and savored and appreciated.

Menu for "A Thing of Beauty Is Forever" Tea

Curried-Tuna-and-Apple Tea Sandwiches • Easy Nut Bread • Passion Fruit Punch

Curried-Tuna-and-Apple Tea Sandwiches

1 6-ounce can solid white albacore tuna, drained
¼ cup finely chopped celery
¼ cup white raisins
2 tablespoons diced onion
1 small Braeburn or Gala apple chopped and dipped in lemon juice
1 small apple thinly sliced
¼ cup mayonnaise
½ teaspoon curry powder
⅛ teaspoon garlic powder
1 tablespoon lemon juice
1 loaf whole-wheat bread

Mix tuna, celery, raisins, onion, and apple together.

In a small bowl, whisk together mayonnaise, curry, garlic, and lemon juice. Pour dressing over tuna mixture and blend together. Spread on each piece of bread (using half a loaf). Add thin slices of apple on top and cover with bread. Trim edges of bread; cut diagonally twice. Arrange on tray.

Easy Nut Bread

(makes 1 large loaf)

3 cups sifted flour
4 teaspoons baking powder
1 teaspoon salt
¾ cup sugar
1 unbeaten egg
1½ cups milk
¼ cup melted shortening
1 cup chopped nuts (your choice)

Sift flour once before measuring. Melt and cool shortening. Grease 8" x 4" loaf pan. Mix together the first four ingredients. Beat the next four items until they are mixed together.

Make a hole in the dry ingredients and pour in

A Touch of Inspiration

In advance of this party, create a list of what makes each woman you have invited beautiful in your eyes. Share these with the group, and encourage others to offer up their words of honor as you lift up each person in attendance.

the liquid mixture. Mix until well blended. Pour the mix into the greased pan. Let stand 20 minutes. Meanwhile, preheat oven to 350° F. Bake for about 1 hour and 10 minutes or until golden brown and firm to the touch. Flavor improves and loaf cuts easier if baked at least a day ahead of time.

Passion Fruit Punch
(makes 8 to 10 servings)

> 5 cups chilled club soda
> 2½ cups frozen passion fruit
>   juice concentrate
>   (measured from 2
>   12-ounce containers),
>   thawedcrushed ice
> fresh mint sprigs

Stir club soda and juice concentrate in pitcher. Pour into tumblers filled with crushed ice. Garnish with mint.

A Role Model Tea

*If I had one gift that I could give you, my friend, it would be
the ability to see yourself as others see you, because only
then would you know how extremely special you are.*

B.A. Billingsly

*W*hat a privilege it is to have people in your life who have been role models. They may be parents, siblings, schoolteachers, coaches, pastors, Sunday school teachers, or even someone you've known only through stories of his or her life. What a gift to host a tea party that honors those people who inspire others to reach new heights of character, perseverance, and faith.

Ask your guests to tell you who they admire and respect as role models. If those people of influence live in the same area, you can invite them to the tea as guests of honor. Have your guests bring and share stories of being mentored or helped by others. Expand your

*At times our own light goes out and is
rekindled by a spark from another person.
Each of us has cause to think with deep
gratitude of those who have lighted the
flame within us.*

ALBERT SCHWEITZER

21

> *There are few hours in life more agreeable than the hour dedicated to the ceremony known as afternoon tea.*
>
> HENRY JAMES

circle by inviting several generations of women. Females of different ages rarely come together. Let the girls, the teens, and the young women get to know the older ladies. Encourage continued conversation between these young ladies and women. This party might be the perfect chance to connect the younger girls with a mentor. It may even inspire future gatherings to keep the dialogue and relationships between generations going.

Through this uplifting time, remember that we are all role models when it comes to showing God's best in all that we do, say, and think.

Menu for a Role Model Tea

Cheese-Nut Sandwiches • Mini Tarts • Almond Punch

Cheese-Nut Sandwiches

8 ounces cream cheese
½ cup milk
½ cup celery, diced
½ cup walnuts, chopped
Whole-wheat bread

Beat 8 ounces of cream cheese until smooth. Thin with about ½ cup of milk, and divide into two equal portions. To one half, mix in ½ cup diced celery and ½ cup chopped walnuts. Spread on whole-wheat bread, top with bread, trim crusts off, cut into squares or diagonal, and place on serving dish. Use rest of cream cheese mixture in next recipe.

Fruit and Cheese Sandwiches

Cream cheese with milk mixture left from previous recipe.

1 cup pineapple bits, finely chopped and drained well
Pumpernickel bread

To the remaining cream cheese mixture from the previous recipe, mix in 1 cup of finely chopped pineapple bits, drained very well. Spread on pumpernickel bread and top with more bread. Trim crusts, cut into squares or diagonal, and place on serving dish.

Mini Tarts

(makes 24)

½ cup softened butter
3 ounces cream cheese, softened
1 cup all-purpose flour
Pecan or Lemon Filling (see below)

Preheat oven to 325° F.

Mix butter and cream cheese. Stir in flour. Roll into 24 1-inch balls. Put balls in ungreased mini muffin tins, and press evenly into the bottom and all the way up the sides of each cup. Fill each with 1 heaping teaspoon of your desired filling (see below).

Bake at 325° F for 30 minutes or until pastry is golden and filling is slightly puffed. Cool slightly in the muffin cups, and then cool completely on a wire rack.

Pecan Filling

1 egg
1 tablespoon melted butter
¾ cup brown sugar
½ cup pecans

Combine ingredients in small bowl until evenly mixed.

Lemon Filling

¼ cup coconut
½ cup sugar
½ teaspoon shredded lemon zest
2 tablespoons melted butter
2 eggs
1 tablespoon lemon juice

Combine ingredients in a small bowl until evenly mixed.

Almond Punch

1 48-ounce can pineapple juice
1 cup sugar
1 cup lemon juice
1 teaspoon pure vanilla extract
1 teaspoon almond flavoring

Mix all ingredients in one-gallon container, and fill the rest of container with water. Chill and serve over ice with garnish.

A Touch of Inspiration

To play on the word "role," you can set your tea table with rolled-up napkins tied with a ribbon or write words of encouragement on small pieces of parchment paper rolled up and tied with a piece of twine or pink ribbon. Place these next to each table setting.

A Memorial Tea

*Both within the family and without, our sisters
hold up our mirrors; our images of who we
are and of who we can dare become.*

Elizabeth Fishell

Celebrate the life of a dear friend or family member who influenced you
greatly but is no longer living. I can't think of anything more intimate and
honoring than sharing favorite memories, photographs, and the enduring
character traits of someone you loved, admired, and knew. When this is done
with the ritual of tea, there is an even deeper sense of tradition and legacy
created for those in attendance.

Invite friends and family, and have
them bring any objects, photos, or uplifting stories about the people who inspired
them or provided love and hope. Have
each guest share why this person of
honor is so special.

Let your guests know ahead of time
that this isn't a time of sorrow, but of celebration. Keep the decorations cheerful
and in light colors. Have photographs

*Teatime is, by its very nature, a
combination of small luxuries
arranged in social symmetry. And
although tea for one is certainly a
fine thing, the addition of a circle of
dear friends to share it with ensures
the whole is larger than its parts.*

AUTHOR UNKNOWN

25

displayed around the room reflecting the person you are honoring. Offer to be the first to share about your special person to break the ice.

Allow plenty of time for your guests to also share. The reflections will be inspiring. Make sure you have Kleenex handy as guests share and hearts are touched. Your guests will leave knowing they have passed along a portion of wisdom, legacy, and humor to others as a tribute to their dear ones.

The influence of one person can shape many lives. As you and your guests honor mentors, may you all be encouraged to reach out to others with kindness and wisdom.

Teatime Delights

If you enjoy the combination of chocolate and mint, heat a cup of milk with a mint tea bag, and then stir in some hot cocoa mix. Garnish with whipped topping.

Menu for a Memorial Tea

Tomato Basil Sandwiches • Emilie's Chocolate Bundt Cake • Spicy Tea

Tomato Basil Sandwiches

(makes 16)

½ cup unsalted butter, cut up

1 teaspoon tomato puree

¼ teaspoon sugar

¼ teaspoon salt

⅛ teaspoon pepper

¼ teaspoon lemon juice

¼ cup lightly packed chopped fresh basil
    or 1 tablespoon dried basil

1 pound fresh tomatoes

8 slices white bread, crusts removed

8 slices whole wheat bread, crusts
    removed

To make the basil butter: Combine butter, tomato puree, sugar, salt, pepper, and lemon juice in a food processor. Process until blended. Add basil leaves. Pulse with on/off turns until blended. Set aside at room temperature.

To make the filling: With a small knife, cut a small cross in bottom skin of each tomato. Place tomatoes into boiling water 20 seconds. Cool in cold water. Drain. Peel, core, and seed tomatoes. Chop tomato flesh very fine. Stir gently in strainer to drain. Just before serving, spread one side of 4 slices of wheat bread and 4 slices of white bread with basil butter. Spread tomato filling on each slice. Season with salt and pepper to taste. Put on top bread. Cut each sandwich in half. Serve fresh.

Emilie's Chocolate Bundt Cake

½ cup sugar
¾ cup water
¾ cup oil
4 eggs
1 small carton sour cream
1 large package chocolate pudding, instant
1 box yellow cake mix
1 12-ounce package chocolate chips
powdered sugar
whipped cream

In a bowl, mix sugar, water, and oil. Mix in remaining ingredients. Pour into oil-sprayed Bundt pan. Bake 350° F for 1 hour. Cool 1 hour and put on cake plate. Top with powdered sugar and whipped cream.

Spicy Tea— An old British recipe

(makes 20 cups)

4 or 5 oranges
5 tablespoons whole cloves
2 cinnamon sticks
2 tablespoons allspice
3 slices fresh ginger
Sugar or honey

Stick whole cloves into the skin of oranges, using about 1 tablespoon for each orange. Roast the oranges for about ½ hour at 350° F, until they become very fragrant. Meanwhile, simmer 2 cinnamon sticks, 2 tablespoons whole allspice, and 3 round slices of fresh ginger in a gallon of water for approximately 10 minutes. Strain out spices. Use the spicy water to brew a gallon of black tea. In a large saucepan, combine the tea and the roasted oranges. Add sugar or honey to taste. Serve hot.

A Touch of Inspiration

Honor today and the future during this tea. Take photos of your gathering with friends, and send each person home with a pretty little frame of remembrance. Tell them you'll send a photo to put into the frame soon. (Don't forget to follow through!) If you have a digital camera and can print the photos at home to include right away, even better!

A friend loveth at all times
Proverbs 17:17

"Words to Live By" Tea

One must spend time in gathering knowledge
to give it out richly.

Edward C. Steadman

Throughout history, people have been sustained by words that bring comfort, wisdom, and inspiration to their hearts and minds. These words are captured in books, sermons, quotes, and greeting cards. Sometimes they are etched only in our memories, very vivid and vital.

This special tea gives you, the hostess, a chance to set the theme around words that have been an inspiration and driving force during different times in your life. Search through various resource materials and have special quotes printed out and randomly placed around the tea setting. Encourage your guests to bring their own words of wisdom to share before, during, and

Kindness is more important than wisdom, and the recognition of this is the beginning of wisdom.

THEODORE RUBIN

after the tea. These bits of wisdom become delightful conversation starters, so allow time for discussion. You'll be amazed at the exchange of ideas. English poet Samuel Taylor Coleridge once wrote, "Common sense in an uncommon degree is what the world calls wisdom." Share a bit of that common sense with the unique charms of a welcoming tea.

Menu for "Words to Live By" Tea

Honey-Smoked Turkey Sandwiches • Butter Cookies • Coconut-Mint Tea

Honey-Smoked Turkey Sandwiches

(serves 10)

2 teaspoons orange juice concentrate
1 teaspoon ginger root, grated
½ cup unsalted butter, softened
1 loaf white bread
½ pound honey-smoked turkey, thinly sliced

Add ginger to juice. In a bowl, whisk together butter and juice. Spread a thin layer of this orange butter on a slice of bread. Place a slice of smoked turkey on top and top with bread. Cut sandwiches into fourths. You can cut using cookie cutters for unique designs.

Butter Cookies

(makes 36)

1 pound butter
1 cup granulated sugar
1 beaten egg
4 cups flour
¼ teaspoon salt
1 tablespoon vanilla

Cream butter and sugar gradually. Add beaten egg. Sift flour and salt together and add to mixture. Stir thoroughly. Add vanilla and mix. Drop dough from teaspoon onto greased cookie sheet. Bake at 350° F for 20 to 25 minutes. May be decorated as desired before or after baking. May also be put through a cookie press.

Coconut-Mint Tea

(makes 8 servings)

2 cups fresh mint leaves
8 cups double-strength fresh-brewed tea
1 cup coconut syrup
5 tablespoons fresh lemon juice

Crush mint leaves with a wooden spoon. Place mint leaves in a large teapot. Add hot tea, coconut syrup, and lemon juice. Add more coconut syrup by tablespoons and add teaspoons of lemon juice to taste if needed.

A Touch of Inspiration

Over tea, invite your guests to discuss how the simplest truths have influenced them the most. Take time to read words of inspiration and wisdom, such as:

Only God can fully satisfy the hungry heart of man (Hugh Black).

We all live with the objective of being happy; our lives are all different and yet the same (Anne Frank).

In art the hand can never execute anything higher than the heart can imagine (Emerson).

I long to accomplish a great and noble task, but it is my chief duty to accomplish humble tasks as though they were great and noble. The world is moved along, not only by the mighty shoves of its heroes, but also by the aggregate of the tiny pushes of each honest worker (Helen Keller).

The perfection of wisdom, and the end of true philosophy is to proportion our wants to our possessions, our ambitions to our capacities, we will then be a happy and a virtuous people (Mark Twain).

If you want to keep your memories, you first have to live them (Bob Dylan).

A Scripture Tea

Wisdom is a tree of life to those who embrace her;
happy are those who hold her tightly.

Proverbs 3:18

On a Sunday afternoon, few things lift one's spirits like a good cup of tea. Pair it with friends, and you have a tea party that will help all your guests begin their week with a dose of inspiration. Since our theme is Scripture, encourage your guests to bring their favorite verses that have gotten them through difficult valleys in their lives. You'll find the sharing time very exciting and uplifting.

Offer to begin and close the time of sharing with a short prayer. This will prepare the hearts and minds of your guests to receive the wisdom offered and to feel God's presence in what is shared and in the gathering itself.

> *Genius is one-percent inspiration and ninety-nine percent perspiration.*
>
> THOMAS EDISON

During my five-months stay in Seattle, Washington, at the Fred Hutchinson's Cancer Research Alliance, I found Scripture very comforting to my spirit. No matter what my situation might be, I can turn to the powerful collection of poetry and praises found in the book of Psalms and know that something appropriate will soothe my soul. Here are some of my favorite verses. May they inspire you to recall the words of Scripture that have meant the most to you in your valleys and moments of victory.

Serve the LORD with reverent fear, and rejoice with trembling…But what joy for all who find protection in him! (Psalm 2:11-12).

35

His favor lasts a lifetime! Weeping may go on all night, but joy comes with the morning (Psalm 30:5).

For you are my hiding place; you protect me from trouble. You surround me with songs of victory (Psalm 32:7).

O God, my heart is quiet and confident. No wonder I can sing your praises! (Psalm 57:7 TLB).

This is the day that the LORD has made. We will rejoice and be glad in it (Psalm 118:24).

Dear friends, let us practice loving each other, for love comes from God and those who are loving and kind show that they are children of God, and that they are getting to know him better (1 John 4:7 TLB).

Menu for a Scripture Tea
Apple Harvest Tea Sandwiches • Pecan Cups • Apple Cider Tea

Apple Harvest Tea Sandwiches

1 8-ounce package softened cream cheese
2 tablespoons brown sugar
½ teaspoon cinnamon
¼ teaspoon nutmeg
1 teaspoon vanilla
1 loaf cinnamon-raisin bread
2 Red or Golden Delicious apples, unpeeled
lemon juice
⅓ cup chopped, roasted, and lightly salted peanuts or walnuts

Combine cream cheese, brown sugar, cinnamon, nutmeg, and vanilla. Beat at medium speed with an electric mixer 1 minute or until smooth. Set aside.

Core apples and slice into thin horizontal slices. Brush with lemon juice.

Spread one side of two slices of bread with cream cheese mixture. Top one slice of bread with apple slices, then place the other slice of bread on top of apples (cream cheese side down). Trim crust off edges. Cut diagonally twice. Lightly spread cheese mixture on front edges. Dip into chopped nuts and arrange on tray.

Pecan Cups
(makes 48)

¾ cup butter, softened
6 ounces cream cheese, softened
2 cups all-purpose flour

Filling
1½ cups packed brown sugar
2 eggs
1 tablespoon butter, melted
48 pecan halves

In a large mixing bowl, cream butter and cream cheese. Gradually add flour, beating until mixture forms a ball. Cover and refrigerate for 15 minutes.

For filling: In a small bowl combine the brown sugar, eggs, and butter. Set aside.

Roll dough into 48 balls. Press onto the bottom and up the sides of greased miniature muffin cups. Spoon a small teaspoon of filling into each cup. Top each with a pecan half. Bake at 350° F for 20 to 25 minutes or until golden brown. Cool for 3 minutes before removing from pans to wire rack to cool.

Apple Cider Tea
(makes 10 cups)

2½ teaspoons black tea leaves
2½ cups boiling water
¼ cup sugar

juice of 2 oranges (about 1 cup)
5 cups apple cider
10 thin lemon slices

Following the traditional method, make tea from tea leaves and boiling water; allow to brew for 5 minutes. Place sugar in a large bowl or pitcher. Strain hot tea into bowl and stir until sugar is dissolved. Stir in orange juice. Just before serving, add apple cider and reheat. Pour into cups and offer slices of lemon. Serve hot or cold.

A Touch of Inspiration

A week after the party or even longer, consider writing a list of some of the favorite scriptures shared during the tea. Make copies of this list and send it to those who attended and to anyone who was unable to attend. Enclose one bag of chamomile, peppermint, or other soothing flavor of tea to inspire a time of reflection.

A Baby Christening Tea

Whoever inquires about our childhood wants to know something about our soul.

Erika Burkhart

𝒯he christening of a child is one of the most precious occasions a family can experience. Most denominations in the Christian faith have their own timing when this event will occur in a child's life. The purpose of a christening is for the parents and family to express their faith and their commitment to raise their child with the tenets of Christianity. The christening might take place at your tea…or the tea may follow the event at the church. However you celebrate this touching occasion, it will be a time of family and spiritual love.

Rejoice in the purity and significance of the event with a lot of white, white, and more white. A few accents of soft color or silver and gold tones

41

can be placed on the tea table in the form of curled ribbon streamers or in the designs on the dishes.

Your guest list will include those family and friends who are willing to dedicate themselves to uphold the child in his or her spiritual journey. Have your guests come with words of encouragement, advice, and godly wisdom for the parents who are raising up this child in the Lord. Give the parents an opportunity to say a few words to those in attendance. This experience might have a rich impact for guests who have never thought about christening or dedicating their children to the Lord. Everyone will be reminded that we are responsible for being examples and encouragers to all children.

A Prayer for a Christening

Father God, what a joy to welcome (baby's name) into our lives. As we look at the miracle of birth and all that it entails, we marvel at Your majesty. This child is a reminder that You are the Creator and we are Your creatures. May You bless this child with good family and friends who come alongside and offer prayer support along the way. We humbly acknowledge that You are the giver of all life. We say *amen* to the christening of this dear child. May this babe remain close to You all through his (her) life and to eternity. Amen.

Menu for a Baby Christening Tea

Crab-and-Olive Sandwiches • Baby's First Chocolate Pecan Bars • Vanilla Milk Tea

Crab-and-Olive Sandwiches
(makes 20)

8 ounces softened cream cheese

¼ pound fresh or frozen crab meat, thoroughly drained

½ cup pitted black olives, drained and chopped

40 slices from French baguette

1 medium cucumber, peeled and cut into 20 thin slices

1 bunch fresh watercress sprigs

1 tablespoon coarsely shredded lemon peel

In a large bowl, beat cream cheese until smooth. Stir in crab meat and olives until well combined.

Spread 1 teaspoon crab mixture onto each bread slice. Top 20 of the bread slices with one cucumber slice and one watercress sprig. Sprinkle lemon peel atop the watercress. Top with remaining bread slices to form sandwiches. You can also leave the top slice of bread off and make them open-faced sandwiches.

Thank God for tea! What would the world do without tea?
How did it exist? I am glad I was not born before tea.

REVEREND SIDNEY SMITH

Baby's First Chocolate Pecan Bars

(makes 48)

1 cup firmly packed light-brown sugar
2 sticks softened butter
1 egg yolk
1 teaspoon vanilla extract
2 cups all-purpose flour
¼ teaspoon salt
1¼ cups semisweet chocolate chunks
½ cup coarsely chopped pecans

Preheat oven to 350° F.

Mix together brown sugar, butter, egg yolk, vanilla, flour, and salt. Spread into a greased 13 x 9-inch pan. Bake for 3 minutes. Remove from oven. Sprinkle chocolate over top, allowing it to melt (about 10 minutes). Spread the melted chocolate evenly with a spatula. Sprinkle nuts over top. Cut bars into 1½-inch squares, and then cut on the diagonal to form triangles.

Vanilla Milk Tea

(makes 4 to 5 cups)
This blend is a perfect introduction for children or for people who aren't accustomed to drinking tea. The amount of milk in the cup can be reduced if the drinker would like a stronger blend of tea. Please use a vanilla bean if at all possible. If that *isn't available, stir in 2 teaspoons of pure vanilla extract into each cup of milk.*

1 cup milk
2-inch piece of vanilla bean, split or
    2 teaspoons pure vanilla extract
4 teaspoons English Breakfast tea
1 quart boiling water

Pour the milk in a small saucepan, add the vanilla bean or extract, and bring to a simmer, stirring often. Remove the pan from the heat and let stand until the milk is cool. Remove the bean from the pan.

Warm a teapot and teacups with hot water. Drain and dry them. Put tea leaves in the teapot and add boiling water. Cover with a cozy or tea towel and let steep for 5 minutes. Pour about ¼ cup of cooled milk into teacups. (You can adjust the amount of milk in each cup depending upon the desired strength of tea.) Stir and strain the tea into the hot cups. Serve right away.

A Touch of Inspiration

It is customary to present the guest of honor with a token gift as a remembrance of this christening tea. If you are celebrating several mothers and children who are honored, present each with a small present—a delicate bud vase of hand-blown glass, a music box, a children's Bible, or an inscribed picture frame to display a photo from the day. Any of these will be a sweet reminder to the parents that as they support their child in the faith, they too are supported by the prayers and love of others.

A Funny Bone Tea

Laughter can relieve tension, soothe the pain of disappointment, and strengthen the spirit of the formidable tasks that always lie ahead.

Dwight D. Eisenhower

When was the last time you laughed until you cried? When was the last time you told a joke? *A Funny Bone Tea* is just what you and your friends need. Start the laughs early by sending invitations with a funny image or a joke you've selected for the person written alongside the teatime information. Encourage your guests to be prepared with funny tales, stories, and jokes. If you want to roll up your sleeves and really get into the fun, suggest a funny theme like a *Topsy Turvy Tea* (upside down), *Be a Clown Day, Pajama Party, Silly Hat Saturday*. Whatever you go with, have your décor and your own attire suit the event!

Our five senses are incomplete without the sixth—a sense of humor. Last year my Bob and I made our theme for the year: "We need to laugh at least once every single day." It's amazing how that opens our eyes to watch for moments of comedy or opportunities to be lighthearted.

Some Laugh Makers

- Worried about an IRS audit? Avoid what's called a red flag. That's something the IRS always looks for. For example, say you have some money left in your bank account after paying taxes. That's a red flag. JAY LENO, *The Tonight Show*
- Two caterpillars were watching a butterfly, when one said to the other, "They'll never get me up in one of those hang gliders." NEIL MCKAY
- Want a good way to keep your house warm? Put a coat of paint on it.
- Sign at a nursing home: "We're not deaf. We've already heard everything worth hearing."
- I use a duck as an alarm clock. It wakes me up at the quack of dawn.
- What do you get when you cross a dog and a hen? You get a pooched egg.
- What did Noah say while he was loading all the animals on the ark? "Now I've herd everything."

Menu for a Funny Bone Tea
Side-Splitting Egg Salad Sandwiches • Funny Bone Cookies • Tickle-Me-Pink Raspberry Iced Tea

Side-Splitting Egg Salad Sandwiches

4 hard-boiled eggs
¼ cup mayonnaise (or use half mayonnaise and half plain yogurt)
1½ teaspoons curry powder
black or green olives
bread

Chop 4 hard-boiled eggs. Mix in ¼ cup of your favorite mayonnaise (or half mayo and half plain yogurt) and 1½ teaspoons curry powder. Garnish with round slices of black or green olives. Make sandwiches. Remove crusts from bread, cut into squares, and arrange on serving tray.

Funny Bone Cookies
(makes 40 to 60)

1 cup granulated sugar
1 cup powdered sugar
1 cup margarine or butter
1 cup salad oil
2 eggs, beaten
1 tablespoon vanilla
5¼ cups flour
1 teaspoon cream of tartar
1 teaspoon baking soda
½ teaspoon salt
powdered sugar

Cream first 4 ingredients. Add eggs and vanilla.

Mix flour, cream of tartar, baking soda, and salt. Add to creamed mixture. Chill. Roll out dough and create cookies with bone-shaped cookie cutter. Sprinkle with sugar. Bake on an ungreased cookie sheet at 375° F for 12 to 15 minutes or until slightly browned.

There is a time for everything, a season for every activity under heaven…
A time to cry and a time to laugh. A time to grieve and a time to dance.

ECCLESIASTES 3:1,4

Tickle-Me-Pink Raspberry Iced Tea

This cold tea drink is refreshing anytime of the year.

6 cups boiling water
½ cup lightly packed fresh mint leaves or
    7 bags of herbal mint tea
4 cups cold water
2 12-ounce containers frozen lemonade
    concentrate
1 cup frozen raspberries

In a teapot, pour boiling water over tea bags; cover and steep 5 minutes. Remove the bags. Place frozen lemonade concentrate in a heatproof pitcher and pour some of the hot mint tea over it. Stir until lemonade is thawed. Pour in rest of tea and stir. Add ice and raspberries before serving.

A Touch of Inspiration

Have a ball with tea! A forerunner of a tea bag, a tea ball is a perforated, ball-shaped metal container. Clasp loose tea inside and place the ball in the pot or cup before the boiling water is poured. Tea balls are not recommended for regular use as they tend to inhibit the full flavor of the tea, but they're convenient—and preferable to a tea bag. And now tea balls come in fun shapes, such as a teapot, and make great gifts or tea favors.

A Book Club Tea

*Books are a delightful society. If you go into a room filled
with books, even without taking them down from their shelves,
they seem to speak to you, to welcome you.*

William E. Gladstone

The environment and geographical setting in a book gives the story a backdrop of history, texture, colors, and the vibrancy of the culture. Why not bring that same rich feel to your next gathering by hosting a *Book Club Tea?* People with many different reading interests enjoy meeting together and connecting over the power of a good story and delicious tea. Plan early so your guests have time to read the selected book.

A clever way to bring a story to life is to create a décor and food theme around the setting of a selected book. If you're reading *Robinson Crusoe,* create an island feel in your living room with plastic or real palm leaves and bright floral arrangements. If you're reading *Christy,* you could turn the space into a charming old schoolhouse. If you're reading a work of Shakespeare, have guests come dressed as a character or prepare a table fit for kings and queens. The possibilities are as endless as the list of

*Books are the quietest and
most constant friends; they
are the most accessible and
wisest of counselors, and the
most patient of teachers.*

CHARLES W. ELIOT

> *Books become as familiar and necessary as old friends. Each change in them, brought about by much handling and by accident only endears them more. They are an extension of oneself.*
>
> CHARLOTTE GRAY

available books to read! Go to your local library for inspiration and loads of information. Other fun tea ideas include an *Alice in Wonderland Tea* or, at Christmastime, *A Christmas Carol Tea* is sure to spark creativity.

In advance of your event, go to your favorite bookstore and see if they have any discount coupons available. If so, ask for one for each of your guests. Hand these out at your tea. This will inspire your friends to invest in a future book for their reading pleasure. Tea is all about friends coming together, and this is the spirit of a book club too. This combined delight will be a time of enjoyable conversation and companionship.

Menu for a Book Club Tea

Salmon-and-Dill Sandwiches • Susie's Oatmeal Chocolate Chip Cookies • Tangerine Tea

Salmon-and-Dill Sandwiches

butter
cream cheese, softened
cream
dill, fresh or dried
smoked salmon or lox
parsley, fresh
bread

Spread the buttered bread with softened cream cheese, which you have thinned with a little cream and flavored with fresh or dried dill weed. Add an ultra-thin slice of smoked salmon or lox. Garnish with fresh dill, if available, or parsley sprig. Trim crusts and cut in squares or at a diagonal. Place and arrange on serving tray.

Susie's Oatmeal Chocolate Chip Cookies

(makes 60)
*Your friends will indeed feel special when they bite
into one of these divine cookies.*

1 cup margarine
1 cup packed brown sugar
1 cup granulated sugar
2 large eggs
1 teaspoon vanilla
1½ cups all-purpose flour
1 teaspoon baking soda
½ teaspoon salt
3 cups uncooked, old-fashioned oatmeal
14 ounces chocolate chips

Preheat oven to 375° F.

In a large bowl, beat margarine until light. Add
sugars and beat until fluffy. Add eggs and vanilla
and beat well. Stir in flour, baking soda, and salt.
Stir in oatmeal and chocolate chips. Use a small
ice cream scoop to drop batter onto an
ungreased cookie sheet. Bake 10 to 12 minutes
until cookies are set. Don't overbake.

Tangerine Tea

7 to 8 teaspoons orange pekoe tea leaves
1 tangerine rind
8 cups boiling water
2 tangerines, cleaned
cloves, whole
cinnamon sticks

Warm teapot with hot water, empty, and dry off.
Add tea leaves and tangerine rind to pot. Pour
boiling water over leaves and rind, and let steep
for 5 minutes. Use a tea cozy to retain heat.

Cut tangerine slices in half and stud with a few
cloves. Place tangerine slices into each teacup
before pouring strained tea. Serve with cinnamon
sticks for stirring. Sweeten with honey or sugar,
if desired.

A Touch of Inspiration

Invite guests by writing party information on a blank bookmark.

Make a centerpiece using stacks of books, flowers, and props that give clues to the book's content.

If you're inviting people who are not friends with each other, use name tags. Cut them out in the
shape of an open book. Use straight pins to fasten onto clothing.

GAIL GRECO, *Tea-Time at the Inn*

More than half a century has passed, and yet each
spring, when I wander into the primrose wood and
see the pale yellow blooms, and smell their sweetest of
scents…for a moment I am seven years old again and
wandering in the fragrant wood.

GERTRUDE JEKYLL

A Garden Tea

*"Just living is not enough," said the butterfly.
"One must have sunshine, freedom,
and a little flower."*

Hans Christian Anderson

A gardener is blessed to experience the deep satisfaction of working side by side with the Creator to develop a place of beauty. There is great joy in working hard and seeing results. There is also a sense of gratitude that takes root when one has even a small role in giving birth to beauty. Toiling in the sun and soil makes the world a better place. Combining this with sharing tea and time with good friends is even lovelier.

Choose spring or early summer to host your *Garden Tea*. Your invitations, decorations, and centerpiece can be made from natural items or inspired by them. If you are fortunate to have a lovely garden, plan the setting nestled under the trees or rose arbor. If weather is fickle in your area, bring the outdoors inside with lots of fresh flowers, potted plants, sunlight, and a sprinkling of leaves and petals. Play a gentle instrumental CD or one that provides the sounds of nature.

If hosting the tea at your place is not convenient or desired, scout out a friend's home, a neighborhood park, a garden club, or even a well-maintained college campus for the perfect spot. Encourage your guests to bring a packet of their favorite flower seeds and have a seed packet exchange as a way for your guests to get to know one another better. Another fun and fruitful idea is to have everyone bring clippings from their favorite plants to share with the group. Each person could walk away with enough plants to start an English garden or vegetable garden or a mix of plants that could start a "friendship" garden.

> *To pick a flower is so much more satisfying than just observing it or photographing it....So in later years I have grown in my garden as many flowers as possible for children to pick.*
>
> ANNE SCOTT-JAMES

God chose a garden as the place of beginnings for mankind. Every time I walk through our garden or visit a friend's, I find renewal. Plant the seeds of friendship with other women, and watch inspiration bloom in brilliant colors.

Menu for a Garden Tea
Chicken Almond Sandwiches • Carrot Cake • Herbal Tea

Chicken Almond Sandwiches

  1 cup cooked chicken, chopped
  ½ cup slivered almonds, toasted
  ½ cup heavy cream
  salt and freshly ground pepper to taste
  8 slices white bread, crusts removed
  8 slices whole wheat bread, crusts removed
  chopped toasted almonds for garnish

In a blender, combine chicken, almonds, heavy cream, salt, and pepper. Blend at low speed until spreadable. Spread one side of each slice of bread with Dijon mustard and butter. Spread chicken filling on half of buttered bread. Add top bread. Cut sandwiches in half. Spread butter along one edge of sandwiches. Press this edge into chopped almonds to garnish.

Carrot Cake

2 cups flour
2 teaspoons baking
   powder
1½ teaspoons baking
   soda
2 tablespoons cinnamon
1 teaspoon salt
2 cups sugar
1½ cups canola oil
4 eggs
2 cups grated carrots
1 cup crushed pineapple, drained
1 cup chopped nuts (pecans or walnuts)

Preheat oven to 350° F. Mix all the ingredients and pour into a 9 x 13 x 2 pan. Bake for 35 to 45 minutes or until toothpick comes out clean.

Butter Cream Icing

1 egg yolk
1 cup butter
8 ounces cream cheese
1 teaspoon vanilla
1 16-ounce box powdered sugar

Beat together all ingredients until smooth. Frost cooled carrot cake.

Herbal Tea

Purchase several kinds of herbal teas that are individually packaged in colorful wrappers. Put a pot of piping hot water on the table with a tray of the teas, allowing guests to choose and prepare their own. Provide honey, cream, and lemon wedges.

A Touch of Inspiration

Adorn your cake or other goodies, such as cupcakes, cookies, or salads, with edible flowers. Here is a list of some of the most popular flowers and their flavors. Be sure to research any others you choose before placing on food items.

- Nasturtium—spicy
- Chives—onion flavor
- Squash, daylily—like a vegetable
- Calendula—buttery
- Mint, pansy—minty
- Sage, marigold—herbal
- Rose, violet—floral

Christmas
Tea

A Christmas Tea

Our hearts grow tender with childhood memories and love of kindred, and we are better throughout the year for having, in spirit, become a child again at Christmastime.

Laura Ingalls Wilder

As long as I can remember, I've set aside the first Saturday in December to host my annual *Christmas Tea*. While I was going through cancer treatments, I didn't host this gathering, and I missed what it brought to my life. What deep joy I felt the Christmas I resumed these gatherings. We'd just moved to our new home near the beach in Southern California. My invitation list had new neighbors and old friends. I was anxious to see how these two groups would blend. Everyone was instant friends. I encourage you to do the same with this tea. Bring together your different groups of friends and coworkers and neighbors in the spirit of Christmas by sharing in fellowship and joy.

For a simple-yet-festive table setting, use a green felt tablecloth as your covering. Add red poinsettias and white candles of various heights as your centerpiece. If children will be there (and even if they won't) a sprinkling of cellophane wrapped peppermint candies add a touch of fun to the table presentation.

Let's be merry; we'll have tea and toast...and an endless host of syllabubs and jellies and mince pies.

PERCY BYSSHE SHELLEY

I have a collection of Christmas cups and saucers stacked on the corner of my table for my guests to personally select which ones they want to use. You may have a full set of one kind or a variety of colors, sizes, and shapes. This is just as lovely and festive. I usually plan a two-hour window for my festive tea. This allows time for introductions, eating, visiting, sharing, and story time. I always find an appropriate new Christmas storybook that can be shared in a few minutes. Each year the ladies can't wait to see what the new tale will be.

Your party doesn't have to be fancy or perfect. The *spirit* of the tea party is what your guests will remember. I like to close the tea with a seasonal prayer such as this one:

O Father, who hast declared Thy love to men by the birth of the Holy Child at Bethlehem; help us to welcome Him with gladness and to make room for Him in our common days; so that we may live at peace with one another and in goodwill with all Thy family; through the same Thy Son, Jesus Christ our Lord. Amen.

WILLIAM BARCLAY, *Prayers for the Christian Year*

Menu for a Christmas Tea
Buttermilk Waffles • Emilie's Snowball Cookies • Christmas Tea (Wassail Bowl)

Buttermilk Waffles
(makes 6 waffles)
These are my Bob's masterpieces.

    2 cups sifted all-purpose flour
    ¼ teaspoon baking soda
    1⅓ teaspoon double-acting baking powder
    1 tablespoon of sugar
    ½ teaspoon salt
    2 eggs, separated, divided use
    1¾ cups buttermilk
    ¾ stick melted butter

Sift flour, baking soda, baking powder, sugar, and salt together.

In separate bowl, beat egg yolks until light. Add and beat together buttermilk and melted butter.

Combine dry and liquid ingredients with a few swift strokes.

Beat egg whites until stiff but not dry and fold gently into batter. Cook in waffle iron per instructions.

Emilie's Snowball Cookies

¾ cup shortening
¾ cup butter
1 cup powdered sugar
3 cups flour
½ teaspoon salt
2 tablespoons vanilla
½ cup chopped nuts (any kind)

Preheat oven to 325° F.

Cream shortening, butter, and ½ cup of the powdered sugar together (set aside other half of powdered sugar). Sift in flour and salt and mix. Add in vanilla and nuts for a final round of mixing. Roll into small balls. Bake for 20 to 25 minutes. While still warm, roll the cookies in the remaining powdered sugar. Coat as thick as you like.

After serving, keep remaining cookies in a tightly sealed container or freeze. These are great to have on hand, especially during the holiday season.

Christmas Tea (Wassail Bowl)

(makes 12 cups)

2 sticks cinnamon
1 teaspoon whole allspice
1 small orange studded with cloves
2 quarts apple juice or apple cider
1 pint cranberry juice

Place cinnamon, allspice, and orange in cheese-cloth. Tie securely. Combine all ingredients in Crock-Pot. Cover and simmer for 5 hours. Serve warm.

A Touch of Inspiration

Make the season extra joyful! When you send the invitations to this *Christmas Tea,* also send your Christmas card and family photo. You'll take care of your Christmas cards early, and the recipients will love the special addition of a party invitation. Invite entire families, and you'll have a house full of childlike wonder and cheer.

Inspiring Tea Reads

by Emilie Barnes
The Twelve Teas of Friendship
The Twelve Teas of Celebration
Friendship Teas to Go

Other Delightful Reads

You're Just My Cup of Tea, Camille Ellerbrook
Tea-Time at the Inn, Gail Greco
A Little English Book of Teas, Rosa Mashiter
Treasuring the Gift of Tea Time, Julie L. Peterson
Country Tea Parties, Maggie Stuckey
The Graceful Art of Tea, Nan Taylor